SCHOLAST

Cursive Writing Practice
WACKY FACTS

By Violet Findley

New York • Toronto • London • Auckland • Sydney
Mexico City • New Delhi • Hong Kong • Buenos Aires

Contents

Cover design by Judith Christ-Lafond
Interior design by Maria Lilja
Illustrations by Doug Jones

ISBN: 978-0-545-94317-8

8 9 10   40   22 21

Introduction

Welcome to *Cursive Writing Practice: Wacky Facts!* In the hustle and bustle of a hectic school day, cursive writing often gets short shrift. With reading, writing, math, science, and social studies to learn, few students have the time or inclination to perfect the fine art of the loop-the-loop. What a shame! Clear cursive writing is one of the best tools available to kids for efficient note-taking and self-expression.

That's where these lively practice pages come in! In as little as five minutes a day, you can spur students to spruce up their cursive writing. Just reproduce and pass out a page, then sit back and watch kids move their pencils with levity and care. Why? Because the simple act of rewriting a wacky fact motivates them to master the shape, size, spacing, slant, and curve of model script.

And here's more good news: The completed practice pages can quickly be bound into an instant wacky-facts book to share with family and friends. Can you think of a cooler way to showcase a child's carefully crafted script? I can't.

Read on to discover more tips for using this resource to improve your students' cursive writing and, in so doing, their essential communication skills.

Your partner in education,

Violet Findley

Using This Resource

This book has been designed for easy use. Before embarking on the wacky-facts pages, it's a good idea to review the basics. Do so by distributing the upper- and lowercase practice pages to students. These sheets include arrows showing the standard way to form each letter in cursive. As students complete these pages, circulate around the room looking for writing "red flags"—that is, kids who are forming their letters in nonstandard ways. If you notice an error, approach the student and model standard formation. This will help students rewire their cursive habits, which will improve both the clarity and speed of their writing down the road.

Once students have reviewed the basics, they're ready to enjoy the wacky-facts pages. These pages can be reproduced in any sequence you choose. Here are some simple routines for sharing them:

Cursive Writing Starters Place a practice page on each student's desk to complete first thing in the morning.

Cursive Writing Center Stock a table with a "practice page of the day" for students to complete independently.

Cursive Writing Homework Send home a page each night for students to complete independently.

Cursive Writing Folders Create personal cursive writing folders filled with photocopies of the pages for students to complete at their own pace.

Making a Wacky-Facts Booklet

Once students have completed their pages, they can follow these simple directions to make a personal wacky-facts booklet. Note: The booklets can comprise as many pages as you like. They need not include every page.

1. Cut the photocopied pages along the dashed lines, discarding the top portions.

2. Optional: Photocopy the blank booklet sheet on page 47 to add original wacky facts to the booklet.

3. Photocopy the booklet cover on page 48.

4. Place the booklet cover on top of the stacked pages in any order you choose.

5. Staple the book along the left-hand side.

6. Color the booklet cover and interior pages.

7. Share the booklet with family and friends.

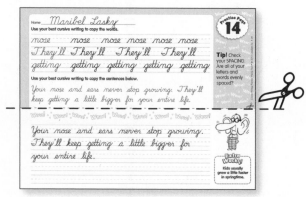

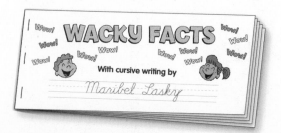

Name _____

Tip! Use the arrows to guide you in forming each letter.

A B C D E F G H I J K L M

N O P Q R S T U V W X Y Z

Use your best cursive writing to copy each letter below.

Extra Wacky!

The praying mantis is the only insect that can turn its head.

Practice Page
Lowercase Letters

Tip! Use the arrows to guide you in forming each letter.

Name _____

a b c d e f g h i j k l m

n o p q r s t u v w x y z

Use your best cursive writing to copy each letter below.

Extra Wacky!

A month that begins on Sunday will always have a Friday 13th.

WED 11
THURS 12
FRIDAY 13

Practice Page 1

Name _____

Use your best cursive writing to copy the words.

Count

Guess

stars

Use your best cursive writing to copy the sentences below.

Count every grain of sand in the entire world.

Guess what? There are still more stars in the sky.

Tip: Check your SIZE. Is each of your letters the right height and resting neatly on the line?

Extra Wacky!

Some huge stars are 100 times bigger than the sun.

Wow! • Wow! • Wow! • Wow! • Wow! • Wow! • Wow! • Wow!

Name _____

Use your best cursive writing to copy the words.

Pizza

breakfast

common

Use your best cursive writing to copy the sentences below.

Pizza for breakfast on a Monday may sound yummy. But

the most common time to eat pizza is dinner on Saturday.

Tip! Check your SLANT. Do all your letters slant in the same direction?

Saturday PIZZA SPecial

Extra Wacky!

In Brazil, they like peas on pizza.

Wow! • Wow! • Wow! • Wow! • Wow! • Wow! • Wow! • Wow!

Name _____

Use your best cursive writing to copy the words.

pencil

words

miles

Use your best cursive writing to copy the sentences below.

To use up a pencil, you could write 50,000 words.

Another way would be to draw a line 35 miles long.

Wow! · Wow! · Wow! · Wow! · Wow! · Wow! · Wow!

I can write lots and lots and lots and and lots and lo !!

Extra Wacky!

A pencil can write underwater.

Name _____

Use your best cursive writing to copy the words.

fingerprints

They

people

Use your best cursive writing to copy the sentences below.

Koalas have fingerprints. They are the only
animals other than people and monkeys that do.

Tip! Check your SPACING. Are all of your letters and words evenly spaced?

Extra Wacky!

Every dog has its own special nose print.

Name _____

Use your best cursive writing to copy the words.

America

bill

President

Use your best cursive writing to copy the sentences below.

America used to have a $100,000 bill. It was the biggest

bill ever and it had a picture of President Woodrow Wilson.

Tip!

Check your
SMOOTHNESS.
Do all of your
letters have
the same line
thickness?

Wow! • Wow! • Wow! • Wow! • Wow! • Wow! • Wow! • Wow!

Wow! • Wow! • Wow! • Wow! • Wow! • Wow! • Wow!

Extra Wacky!

It costs nearly
2 cents to make
each penny!

Tip! Clear your desk so you have room to write.

Name

Use your best cursive writing to copy the words.

Raindrops

hamburger

round

Use your best cursive writing to copy the sentences below.

Raindrops are not shaped like drops. They are shaped like

hamburger buns. Raindrops are round on top, flat on bottom.

Wow! • Wow! • Wow! • Wow! • Wow! • Wow! • Wow!

Extra Wacky!

Umbrellas used to be called bumbershoots.

Wow! • Wow! • Wow! • Wow!

Name _____

Use your best cursive writing to copy the words.

left

faster

on

Use your best cursive writing to copy the sentence below.

If you are left handed, your fingernails grow a little bit faster on your left hand than on your right.

Wow! • Wow! • Wow! • Wow! • Wow! • Wow! • Wow! • Wow!

LEFT

RIGHT

Extra Wacky!

Left Handers Day is celebrated each year on August 13.

Name

Use your best cursive writing to copy the words.

study

child

laugh

Use your best cursive writing to copy the sentences below.

According to a study, the average child laughs 300

times each day. Adults laugh only 17 times a day.

Tip! Practice your cursive writing a little each day.

HA! HA! HA!

Extra Wacky!

Rats laugh when they're tickled.

Name _____

Use your best cursive writing to copy the words.

The

crawling

planet

Use your best cursive writing to copy the sentences below.

The Earth is crawling with bugs. For every

person on the planet, there are 200 million insects.

Tip! For extra practice, copy your favorite quotes in cursive.

Wow! • *Wow!* • *Wow!* • *Wow!* • *Wow!* • *Wow!* • *Wow!* • *Wow!*

Extra Wacky!

On earth, there are about twice as many chickens as people.

Practice Page

10

Tip! Always take your time and do your best.

Name _____

Use your best cursive writing to copy the words.

record

to

hiccups

Use your best cursive writing to copy the sentences below.

The world record for hiccuping belongs to Charles Osborne. The poor man had the hiccups for 68 years.

Wow! • Wow! • Wow! • Wow! • Wow! • Wow! • Wow!

Hiccup!

Extra Wacky!

Boys get hiccups more than girls.

Name _____

Use your best cursive writing to copy the words.

silly

people

bike

Use your best cursive writing to copy the sentences below.

A super silly tandem bicycle was created that could seat

35 riders. That's like a busload of people on one bike.

Wow! Wow! Wow! Wow! Wow! Wow! Wow! Wow! Wow!

Cursive Writing Practice: Wacky Facts • © Scholastic Inc. • 17

Tip! Check your SIZE. Is each of your letters the right height and resting neatly on the line?

Extra Wacky!

The very first bikes didn't have pedals. You just scooted along.

Practice Page 12

Name _____

Use your best cursive writing to copy the words.

Nearly

field

happened

Use your best cursive writing to copy the sentences below.

Nearly 9,000 people made snow angels in a big field at the same time. That happened in North Dakota in 2007.

Tip! Check your SLANT. Do all your letters slant in the same direction?

Extra Wacky!

The largest snowflake ever measured was more than one foot wide!

Wow! • Wow! • Wow! • Wow! • Wow! • Wow! • Wow! • Wow! • Wow!

Name _____

Use your best cursive writing to copy the words.

group

hyena

called

Use your best cursive writing to copy the sentences below.

A group of hyenas is called a cackle. A group of mice is called a mischief. And a group of cobras is called a quiver.

Wow! • Wow! • Wow! • Wow! • Wow! • Wow! • Wow! • Wow! • Wow!

HA HA HA HA

Extra Wacky!

A group of porcupines is called a prickle.

Name _____

Use your best cursive writing to copy the words.

nose

They'll

getting

Use your best cursive writing to copy the sentences below.

Your nose and ears never stop growing. They'll keep getting a little bigger for your entire life.

Tip! Check your SPACING. Are all of your letters and words evenly spaced?

Wow! Wow! Wow! Wow! Wow! Wow! Wow! Wow!

Extra Wacky!

Kids usually grow a little faster in springtime.

Name _____

Use your best cursive writing to copy the words.

women

chameleons

tiny

Use your best cursive writing to copy the sentences below.

In the 1800s, women wore live chameleons as jewelry. They'd attach the lizards to their dresses with a tiny leash and collar.

Tip!

Check your SMOOTHNESS. Do all of your letters have the same line thickness?

Wow! • Wow! • Wow! • Wow! • Wow! • Wow! • Wow!

Extra Wacky!

If a lizard loses its tail, the tail can grow back.

Name _____

Use your best cursive writing to copy the words.

Two

state

course

Use your best cursive writing to copy the sentences below.

Two cities have the same name as their state. There's Maine, Maine, and, of course, New York, New York.

Tip! Clear your desk so you have room to write.

WELCOME TO MAINE

MAINE

Extra Wacky!

There's a town named Boring in Oregon.

Name _____

Use your best cursive writing to copy the words.

invented

Several

athletes

Use your best cursive writing to copy the sentences below.

The high-five was invented in the 1970s. Several different

pro athletes have taken credit for this handy gesture.

Tip! If you have to break a word at the end of the line, use a hyphen.

Extra Wacky!

The world record for clapping is 1,020 times in a minute.

Tip! Practice your cursive writing a little each day.

Name

Use your best cursive writing to copy the words.

Buzz

female

sting

Use your best cursive writing to copy the sentences below.

Buzz, buzz! Bet you didn't know that only female bees sting and only female mosquitoes drink blood.

Extra Wacky!

Male seahorses carry babies.

Wow! Wow! Wow! Wow! Wow! Wow! Wow! Wow!

Tip! For extra practice, copy your favorite quotes in cursive.

Name _____

Use your best cursive writing to copy the words.

fluffy

cloud

elephants

Use your best cursive writing to copy the sentence below.

Clouds may look light and fluffy, but the water in a single cloud can weigh as much as 100 elephants!

Wow! Wow! Wow! Wow! Wow! Wow! Wow! Wow! Wow!

Extra Wacky!

A bolt of lightning could toast 100,000 pieces of bread.

500 TONS

Name _____

Use your best cursive writing to copy the words.

million

exact

birthday

Use your best cursive writing to copy the sentences below.

About 20 million people in the world have the exact same birthday as you. That's a lot of candles!

Wow! • Wow! • Wow! • Wow! • Wow! • Wow! • Wow! • Wow!

Tip! Always take your time and do your best.

HAPPY BIRTHDAY TO ME AND YOU AND YOU AND —YOU AND YOU...

Extra Wacky!

August is the most common month for birthdays.

Name _____

Use your best cursive writing to copy the words.

first

baby

How

Use your best cursive writing to copy the sentences below.

When it's first born, a baby panda is teeny tiny.

It is even smaller than a mouse. How cute!

Tip! Check your SIZE. Is each of your letters the right height and resting neatly on the line?

Extra Wacky!

Pandas have six fingers on each paw.

Name _____

Use your best cursive writing to copy the words.

Blue

weren't

They

Use your best cursive writing to copy the sentences below.

Blue jeans were invented in the 1800s, but they weren't
called that at first. They were called "waist overalls."

Tip! Check your SLANT. Do all your letters slant in the same direction?

Extra Wacky!

The first jeans didn't have belt loops because people used suspenders.

Wow! Wow! Wow! Wow! Wow! Wow! Wow! Wow! Wow!

Tip! Check your SHAPE. Are all of your letters the right shape and closed where they should be?

Name _____

Use your best cursive writing to copy the words.

sentence

letter

alphabet

Use your best cursive writing to copy the sentence below.

This sentence uses every letter in the alphabet:

"The quick brown fox jumps over the lazy dog!"

Wow! • Wow! • Wow! • Wow! • Wow! • Wow! • Wow! • Wow! • Wow!

Extra Wacky!

No U.S. state has the letter Q in its name.

Name _____

Use your best cursive writing to copy the words.

muscles

bodies

Grasshoppers

Use your best cursive writing to copy the sentences below.

People have 639 muscles in their bodies. Does that sound

like a lot? Not to grasshoppers. They have 900 muscles!

Wow! • Wow! • Wow! • Wow! • Wow! • Wow! • Wow! • Wow! • Wow!

Practice Page
24

Tip! Check
your SPACING.
Are all of your
letters and
words evenly
spaced?

Extra Wacky!

An ant can lift
something
100 times
its weight.

Name _____

Use your best cursive writing to copy the words.

Ready

sport

plastic

Use your best cursive writing to copy the sentences below.

Ready, set, roll! Zorbing is a sport where you roll down a hill inside a big plastic ball. Wheeeeeeee!

Wow! • Wow! • Wow! • Wow! • Wow! • Wow! • Wow!

Extra Wacky!

In the old days, tug of war was a sport in the Olympics.

Name _____

Use your best cursive writing to copy the words.

The

computers

size

Use your best cursive writing to copy the sentences below.

The first computers were made in the 1940s. They couldn't fit on a desk. They were the size of a room!

Tip! Clear your desk so you have room to write.

Extra Wacky!

Scientists recently created a microscopic guitar.

Wow! • Wow! • Wow! • Wow! • Wow! • Wow! • Wow! • Wow!

Name _____

Use your best cursive writing to copy the words.

impossible

eyes

you'll

Use your best cursive writing to copy the sentences below.

Achoo! It is nearly impossible to sneeze with your eyes wide open. Try it next time and you'll see.

Tip! If you have to break a word at the end of the line, use a hyphen.

ACHOO!

Extra Wacky!

It is impossible to cry in outer space.

Wow! Wow! Wow! Wow! Wow! Wow! Wow!

Name _____

Use your best cursive writing to copy the words.

have

teeth

into

Use your best cursive writing to copy the sentences below.

Snails have teeth, lots of them. They can have as

many as 25,000 teeth packed into their tiny mouths.

Tip! Practice your cursive writing a little each day.

Extra Wacky!

The toothbrush was invented in China in 1498.

Wow! • Wow! • Wow! • Wow! • Wow! • Wow! • Wow!

Name _____

Use your best cursive writing to copy the words.

Of

name

favorite

Use your best cursive writing to copy the sentence below.

If you asked people around the world, more would name blue as their favorite color than any other.

Wow! Wow! Wow! Wow! Wow! Wow! Wow!

Blue   Bleu   Lánsè

Extra Wacky!

The color yellow makes people hungry.

Practice Page 30

Tip! Always take your time and do your best.

Extra Wacky!

President John Quincy Adams had a pet alligator.

Name _____

Use your best cursive writing to copy the words.

President

read

daughter

Use your best cursive writing to copy the sentences below.

President Barack Obama read all seven Harry Potter books. He read them with his daughter Malia.

Wow! • Wow! • Wow! • Wow! • Wow! • Wow! • Wow! • Wow! • Wow!

Tip! Check your SIZE. Is each of your letters the right height and resting neatly on the line?

Name _____

Use your best cursive writing to copy the words.

means

backwards

forwards

Use your best cursive writing to copy the sentences below.

"Dr. Awkward" is a palindrome. That means it reads the same way backwards and forwards.

Wow! • Wow! • Wow! • Wow! • Wow! • Wow! • Wow! • Wow!

drawkwarD

Dr. Awkward

Extra Wacky!

No words rhyme with month, orange, silver, or purple.

Name _____

Use your best cursive writing to copy the words.

Open

four

hippopotamus

Use your best cursive writing to copy the sentences below.

Open up and say "Aaaaaa." If you are four feet tall,
you can stand in the open mouth of a hippopotamus.

Extra Wacky!

A newborn hippo weighs about 50 pounds.

Tip! Check your SLANT. Do all your letters slant in the same direction?

Name

Use your best cursive writing to copy the words.

cold

Niagara

huge

Use your best cursive writing to copy the sentences below.

Brrrrr! Sometimes it gets so freezing cold that

Niagara Falls is completely covered in huge icicles.

Tip! Check your SHAPE. Are all of your letters the right shape and closed where they should be?

BRRRR...

Extra Wacky!

The Popsicle™ was invented in 1905 by an 11-year-old boy.

Wow! Wow! Wow! Wow! Wow! Wow! Wow! Wow! Wow!

Name _____

Use your best cursive writing to copy the words.

Smile

different

expressions

Use your best cursive writing to copy the sentences below.

Smile for the camera and say, "Arf!" Did you know

a dog can make about 100 different facial expressions?

Extra Wacky!

A human can make 10,000 facial expressions.

Name _____

Use your best cursive writing to copy the words.

Everything

shoelaces

called

Use your best cursive writing to copy the sentences below.

Everything has a name, even the little plastic tubes at the end of shoelaces. They are called "aglets."

Tip!
Check your SMOOTHNESS. Do all of your letters have the same line thickness?

Extra Wacky!
The metal part of a pencil is called a "ferrule."

Wow! Wow! Wow! Wow! Wow! Wow! Wow!

Practice Page 36

Name _____

Use your best cursive writing to copy the words.

Ketchup

medicine

upset

Use your best cursive writing to copy the sentences below.

Ketchup was first invented as a medicine.

People used it to help cure an upset stomach.

Wow! Wow! Wow! Wow! Wow! Wow! Wow! Wow! Wow!

Tip! Clear
your desk so
you have room
to write.

Extra Wacky!

Snail syrup was
an old-time cure
for sore throats.

Name _____

Use your best cursive writing to copy the words.

Elephants

jump

sloths

Use your best cursive writing to copy the sentences below.

Elephants can't jump. There are many other animals

that also can't jump, including sloths and rhinoceroses.

Cursive Writing Practice: Wacky Facts • © Scholastic Inc. • 43

Tip! If you have to break a word at the end of the line, use a hyphen.

Extra Wacky!

Chickens can only fly for about 10 seconds.

Wow! Wow! Wow! Wow! Wow! Wow! Wow! Wow!

Wow! Wow! Wow! Wow! Wow! Wow! Wow! Wow!

Name _____

Use your best cursive writing to copy the words.

average

twenty

asleep

Use your best cursive writing to copy the sentences below.

On average, it takes a ten-year-old child about

twenty minutes to fall asleep at night. Zzzzzzzzzz!

Wow! Wow! Wow! Wow! Wow! Wow! Wow! Wow!

Extra Wacky!

People have about five dreams per night.

Name _____

Use your best cursive writing to copy the words.

bubble
_____

pink
_____

favorite
_____

Use your best cursive writing to copy the sentences below.

Why is bubble gum usually pink? Pink was the

favorite color of the man who invented it in 1928.

Tip! For extra practice, copy your favorite quotes in cursive.

THINK PINK!

Extra Wacky!

Thousands of years ago people chewed bark as gum.

Wow! • Wow! • Wow! • Wow! • Wow! • Wow! • Wow!

Name _____

Use your best cursive writing to copy the words.

If

growing

newborn

Use your best cursive writing to copy the sentences below.

If you kept growing as fast as you did as a newborn, you'd weigh about 400,000 pounds at age 10. Wow!

Tip! Always take your time and do your best.

Wow! Wow! Wow! Wow! Wow! Wow! Wow! Wow!

SIZE
6 xxxxxx
xxxxxx
XXXXL

Extra Wacky!

On the moon, you would weigh only about 10 pounds.

Wow! • Wow! • Wow! • Wow! • Wow! • Wow! • Wow! • Wow! • Wow! • Wow! • Wow!

Wow! • Wow! • Wow! • Wow! • Wow! • Wow! • Wow! • Wow! • Wow! • Wow! • Wow!

Booklet Covers Photocopy this page and cut along the dashed lines to create two booklet covers.

Wow! Wow! Wow! Wow!

Wow! Wow!

WACKY FACTS

Wow! Wow!

Wow! Wow! Wow!

With cursive writing by

Wow! Wow! Wow! Wow!

Wow! Wow!

WACKY FACTS

Wow! Wow!

Wow! Wow! Wow!

With cursive writing by